WISDOM'S IN THOUGHTS OF

TABLE OF CONTENTS

1. Who Am I
2. When It Comes
3. The Thoughts of Her
4. Night Thoughts
5. The Invitation
6. Lean In
7. It's Already Won
8. In The Heart of Me Hear
9. The Wedding Ring
10. How I See Her
11. What Will I Find
12. Did You Imagine?
13. Special
14. Covenant
15. Everlasting
16. A Marriage Song
17. Foundations

18 Sacrifices

19 Wisdom

20 Anointing And Authority

21 What Next

22 In The Midnight Hour

23 Heartbeats

24 The Chamber

25 More Than Just Words

26 His

27 I See The Time

28 Intimately

29 I Tried To Know

30 Consummat

31 Our Wedding Night

32 Our Wedding Ring

33 Special

WHO AM I

Well it's Monday morning and to me it's clear,
You have reached my heart;
Even though you are there and I am here,
I know our life together is to but a start:

You call my name and I respond to your voice,
Why do I hear your hearts beat?
Because I hear in your call, your desire so sweet,
And to respond to you, is my sacred choice:

The days ahead say to me and I pray to you,
Expect my greatness to come because I'm true;
I am deliberate with grace that ministers hope,
And faithful to reveal my certainty:

That I'm doing; yes to my fullest scope
So abide the process and focus on me:

Who am I and what do I bring?
I am He who pleads.........
I am He who shows.........
I am He who sings.........
I am He who goes...........
I am He who speaks to your needs..........
I am He whose breath on you blows........
I am your vision and all that you can know.......
I am love.......

_____
_____
_____
_____
_____
_____
_____

When it comes.

I think to myself that the time is come,

It's a time to move ahead;

What's the mission and what's the cause,

I hear Holy Spirit. And the things he said.:

Shall I stand in this place or shall I pause,

To do his will absent of any flaw,

And by his spirit. I am LED.:

I see his gift and grace to me.,

and it's love expressed and given.;

She's marked as I, the vision to see,

And her heart with mine now is driven.;

How will we do this work of the Spirit??

How will we fulfill the task?

It's not a time of need to fear it...

It will be unveiled and have no mask;

So we walk In it; the love of God;

A glorious tool;

We unwrap the mystery of the sod,

As he winds us in His holy spool;

To accomplish for him without breaking stride,

You and I, the image of those tried;

without arrogance, Unto him we cried,

As we are become one, the Groom and the Bride.

_____
_____
_____
_____
_____
_____
_____
_____
_____
_____
_____
        _____

THE THOUGHT OF HER
(WISDOM)

I thought of her again today,

We talked through the night;

She said many things to make me think,

I was a better man when I came away:

I realized the truth in what she had to say,

She helped free me from the inner fights;

In her refreshing waters, I did drink,

The truth did change me; I have a new sway:

So back to the places of focused thought,

Into the arms of counsel wrought;

I find the ways of His heart, in her special intrigues,

A friendship of spirit, in kindred mysteries;

Who but the Wise God, who my soul bought,

Would consider me in so wise a thought;

I love His power and how my heart He reads,

Just one of many stirrings; a new and special breed:

Thus now in the very heat of this matter,

Every broken place healed, my bones made fatter;

For the words of His heart cuts through the deep places,

With surgical skill and meticulous precision removed the traces;

Of brokenness and wounds of impassioned pain,

She settles my hurts and lifts the stains:

I believe the gift is given me,

To walk this world completely free;

I will not chide the blessing given,

But have a full life that's Spirit driven:

Show more of her I will plead,
Even the thought of her by name;
Will stir again the fires of my love,
Because in her I find no shame:

Who is she and what's her decree?
How is she so skilled?
How does she see?
How has she become so glory filled?

Leaving herself in the unfolding,
Many tremendous truths that bring understanding;
to the foolish heart you find her scolding,
While setting up tapestry and booths,
Wisdom and instruction revealing her truths:

I must have her, for she is my delight,

And after her I will pursue;

I will embrace her and be loved by her in the night,

for the fire of her warmth is true:

I will speak her name with tender desire,

and from her flame she will warm me;

I will give myself to her and retire.

From all that is death to her quality;

So now let her come forth, and love me gentle;

I will keep her every covenant

I know Her blood over my doorposts and lentils,

She will love me tenderly and sweetly;

innocently. I am measured, intently,

And her voice in my heart speaks gently:

I will confess my love to her,

And say all that's in my heart;

Again, O' lover, stir me and cove

And let us never part......

NIGHT THOUGHTS

Please don't turn away, I'm coming to rest;

All night I struggled in the thoughts of my head,

What was wrong that we didn't talk?

I lie awake at night wrestling with what wasn't said.

Why did you not answer? And what made you balk?

Was there something I said? Or did; Something I sought?

That kept me awake and made me walk:

Yet I asked the question and I call for wisdom,

It puzzles me and I don't understand,

You are so sensitive to hear the things that I've planned;

So tell me, have I taken too much for granted?

Has it cost me all the seed I've planted?

In your heart, a part of me still lives,

I hope for the harvest that time will give:

So is it too much; a difficult task?
To speak with me is all I ask.

My heart will hear what you have to say,

I hope from me you won't turn away;

knowing that I'm caught in the thoughts of my day:

Please don't Turn away.

_____
_____
_____
_____
_____
_____
_____
_____
_____
_____ ---

THE INVITATION

I thought to myself just then,
What a whirling, spinning, twirling
Circumstances of before, and yesterday when,
Conditions were different and waters swirling:

I didn't know the things I know now,
How different I was back then,
So young and foolish in how I trow;
Then, years later, I have to mend;

Heal The heart of me, every tender place;
Breaking the mold for a treasured space;
To gain more relevant Sensibilities;
And to pursue with the Spirit; Christ's glorious delicacies;

Can I win them and gain a field of great price?
Purchase through a focused heart,

Or do I pause to consider more?

And wait for him to start:

To show me again what he has in store,

Then I realized that this is my station;

This is my given core,

To go for it now; I have his invitation.

LEAN IN

I said to Her (wisdom) in the discussion led;

A question She has asked of me;

Will you give yourself to the things that you hear?

Will you in fact know the worth of what is said?

Will you lean in?

Lean in, you say, with no frustration;

To receive what's spoken without fear,

when thoughts of purpose beyond my head,

Call you to change and trust and then:

To do what I can in the hand of another,

Knowing there is much to do,

To walk the path Yet untrodden, to go further;

Yes, further than I wanted to?

Lean in you say, that's the battle?

And how do I win this fight?

I cannot stay here on the fence, that I Do straddle;

I must face the call, My plight:

It's good You see, the spirits call,

His cry so desperate within me;

The warfare that brings the constant brawl,

To lean in and trust his wisdom free:

To lean in, I say, and face the challenge,

and fight the fight of faith.,

To endure the change and keep the balance,

Following at his motivated pace:

Yes, to be stirred by Her and not by me.,

To keep the straight and narrow wind;

Something inside of me does leap,

And I am still motivated; compelled: To lean in.

IT'S ALREADY WON

I thought through the day, things that have been.,

All the words expressed and what they mean;

So much to consider, the standard of HIM,

How do we live his word That's seen?

No more, just speaking things left undone;

We're expecting something that remains unspoken;

But pursuit of victories, yet to be won,

And kept words, no promises, broken:

What and how to do all that's said,

Walking in covenant, with daily bread;

Entering and leaving the presence of him,

fellowship, works, given; completing them:

This will do with gracious help,

obediently settled in our course;

Taking prey as the lions. Whelp., Establishing the Kingdom with righteous force:

Nothing shall stop the fountain of his blood,
Shed for the causes of men;
What shall prevent salvations flood?
Absolutely nothing, the adversary can send;
For God has already given His Word: His Son.
And assured our blessing; we've already won.

IN THE HEART OF ME
(All will be revealed)

I think of her in the heart of me;
In hidden places; Not any have touched;
A place of depths, that few can see,
My place of strength, A sacred crutch;

How I have longed to see my desire,
To ignite the kindling, to spark The fires;
To express with words, the total sum
And feel its warmth, as new love has come:
She speaks her words to the deep in me
She caresses my spirit, with such intensity;
I reached for her in my mind's eye,
and when I feel her, my heart cries

It cries out with passion for the touch of her,
She drips with honey and the scent of myrrh;

I would she come with hasty feet
Bringing me kisses of love, so fresh. so sweet;

I remember then the time appointed,
And embrace my portion: She's God's anointed;
So I don't allow my thoughts to proceed,
For I am comforted, faithful to let the Spirit lead;

I'll wait for my change with bated breath,
And sorrow not as those who left;
I pursue Her still with expectancy,
Because in time, my beloved, shall be revealed in me!

I nurture the promise and endure the trial,
I praise and give thanks, I keep my smile;
What a place of grace, I say,
I will See it's end one glorious day;

I will be in adventure and mystery,

Opening the packages she's given to me;

I will love every moment and remember with pause.;

That God honored me in His righteous cause.

I give Him praise, but he gives me favor,

Now to enjoy Wisdom's Special Flavor;

So in my heart I think her true,

That the day is soon, all things new;

With this then I wait and wait,

for the time will come when I enter His gates;

I'll come with singing and laughter too;

because all will be revealed, As new flavors; We brew.

_____
_____
_____
_____
_____
_____
_____
_____

_____

_____

_____

_____

OUR WEDDING RING

Small the band a circle precious,

Gold or silver, our wedding ring;

Having. jewels that speak of glorious intent,

A sound, a tone that rings:

Curious that sound a circular moment;

Symphony of orchestration and dance,

Two hearts united, to give forth a clear sound of Oneness....

Their will and spirits lanced:

A set together. One operation;

A man, A woman, Addition or multiplication?

The character; Quality? Special;

Whose perceptions rang true;

A bell; A chime? With moments ringing;

each one God breathed and new:

The ring which leads in course….a circle,

The unctions gentle and sweet;

A holy union before God and man,

A wonderous journey to complete:

So with all desire, and holy vision,

With grateful heart for new days ahead;

While breaking the hymen and circumcisions;

She can only know truly and free,

And Her heart involved in a way, her only to be;

Nothing hidden, no devices, no deceit;

Only loves eyes and thoughts complete:

She's a treasured crown; jeweled and bright,

A spirit renewed and refreshed in the light;

I tell Her in wonder truly,

For on Her is made a gown of radiant beauty:

Set in one with soft dove eyes,

A storied truth, that gives no lies;

With all that comes in purpose sweet,

I trod with joy Her love to meet!

_____
_____
_____
_____
_____
_____
_____
_____
_____
_____
        _____

WHAT WILL I FIND

I pause to consider so many times,

what I would say that could reveal our rhyme;

Well. Occasions of us, you and me;

With gracious events and specialties:

What will it take to give thunderous expressions,

to the valuable rhythms of song and syncopations;

That thought weak given greater expectations.,

Honored in greater emphasis and revelation;

It queries me., these times wondered at;

To know the depths of their special fact:

What looked on the surface to be without merit,

holds fast my attention, and in strength I bear it;

The changes of the rhythm of my heart, beat;

To a new exciting sound that repeats;

To me so much the intimated desire,

which calls me near to your Fervor and fire:

What will it cost to seek your secrets hidden?

I hear your call and I know I'm bidding;

I suspect your depth to be great for me,

Yet, to inquire of you, my own heart Pleads:

I think Yet again, what mysteries lie,

Can I afford the time to try?

I can't but help to pursue what I will,

I must discover and continue still;

For what I know is this very thing;

that no matter what her mysteries bring;

I do for her with all my heart, seek,

So I press in and let life course speak:

Her wisdoms and graces each day removed,

and without measure walk straightly true:

No Fear of failure and absolutely no doubt,

Her heart will show me what she's all about:

And in this process, I'll not at all fear,

What my soul can experience in having Her near;

I will simply trust that in you there's a release,

and pleasantly discover my hearts peace.

_____
_____
_____
_____
_____
_____
_____
_____
_____
_____
_____

DID YOU IMAGINE

Noticing in my mind's eye a consistent pattern,

As though my soul opened to revelations Lantern;

A familiar thought and I stood provoked,

as I gaze upon the words you spoke:

I looked into them with the depths of me,

I thought that it was a place that no one could see;

How could you know what commanded my heart?

And express concerns to my inward parts?

What to the naked eye did not appear?

Yet you focused in with Starry Gaze so near;

Touching the broken and seeing the nicks,

Dinged by life circumstances and a need to be fixed:

You did not shy away and hide your face,

But Cain beside me to stand in this place;

A place of relationship abandoned by others,
To land your love and to help your brother;

And what has happened, In the midst of all this?
Did you know that it would take an unexpected twist?
Did you see the turn and the change that would come?
Did you ever believe that you would be the one?

To stand with me in such a new setting,
Then experience the dawn of new love, begetting;
A wonderful romance in hopes new grace,
Settling old covenants and quickening new pace:

To speed up the time on assignments for you,
With loves, sweet taste and delight, Of covenant made new;
Will you travel with me, this new road?
And go the way together that we've never trode?

Can you suspect the blessings ahead of us dear?

Do you feel the light of joy and wonder so near;

A brand new place of hopes, expectation;

Longed for by all from the time of creation:

Did you know or think of a life of new passion?

Did you once consider it, or ever imagine?

To care and to be cared for is the breath of Glee,

as we take up to the end: Loves Jubilee!

You dear love believe all things and hope all things,

And in Wisdoms challenge, more courage you bring;

So my soul delights in you to care,

In joy most hopeful, great grace to bare!

_____
_____
_____
_____
_____

SPECIAL

How can I say what is happening in my heart?

What words are there, that can tell?

I tried to speak and say my part,

and with reserve, try not to yell:

And what shall I say that can express my thoughts?

The intimate works of me To you?

The desires I have and how I've fought;

How can I prove that that they are true?

I care so deeply for the one I see,

With life, eyes wide open and clear;

And the churning of my spirit, and the words that flee,

And how I'm longing to have you near:

O' Holy Spirit, somehow, I must find a way.,

And do with the sum of me;

Speak to you each and every day,

To receive your love and care and friendship made free;

So let me say now what's in my heart,

Can I know for certain what you will impart;

To me, an evidence that you've heard my words,

and will not chide or sneer.. With despondent chords;

As though I have missed the center mark,

in trying to convey what whispers in my heart;

Or be foolishly impassioned without a vigorous call,

Or compel you no more, as with my love to enthrall;

Still, I take up my cause with radiant passion,

to pursue you yet, in aggressive fashion;

Refusing to be let away without saving,

My friendship with you and appropriately behaving;

And in the end of this mystery,

Loads full intent; To gain precious victory,

So think it not strange in the pursuits of me,

That at the end of this time, you and me will be,

COVENANT

What can I say of this agreement? Binding,

The thought of it compelling, as so I'm Finding;

It's effects on parties, In Solemn contract;

A vow of faith and promise, an endearing compact;

All who are called to it must agree,

It costs our severe, for it comes not free;

The price of that, which makes its demand,

On all who make promises and then won't stand;

Call to walk in a life accord,

The state of being agreed as one, total concord;

What to expect the method of action?

Consummated Faith, and extended protraction;

So how long does a covenant run?

As long as the terms written and agreed upon;

But who can say, I promise, and so take a wife,
and Fail not to do, what's said in life;

Can our words be lost because we selfishly vent,
and fall to confusions, not doing what's meant;
Do we expect to live in denial un-agreed?
When truth is the only thing that makes us free:

I think not these ways to be the original intent,
Of what was purposed in vision sent;
But God's heart known and his words spoken,
with total commitment and covenant unbroken.

So how can we do and then not keep?
Union and faithfulness to the words we speak;
Wisdom demands an audience of witness,
And what we do, speaks of our fitness:

Is not our obedience to the agreement, our burden?

Can it be lifted merely because we are hurting?
Do the tears in my eyes give me a free course,
Shall I leave off the mandate of it with no remorse?

Who shall say that I am free to do as I please?
Who shall set the order for me to appease?
My thoughts and not the thoughts of him,
To justify me is folly and to declare me free at a whim:
But I say to you and believe it's all true.,
No man nor I, can change what God said we must do;
Come then, and let us reason in his word,
to cry foul because of circumstance, is really absurd;
We are judged in our submission to His words sent,
Knowing this then, It's all about His covenant.

_____
_____
_____
_____
_____
_____

EVERLASTING

Having spent some time in recent days,

Finding the need to change my ways;

Needing to look with introspect,

At all the things I tried to protect:

Chiefly me from the things around me,

Changes in life that try to drown me;

Much Ado, about nothing I fear,

I seek then one whose words draw me near:

I claim His wisdom for use, You see,

Because the knowledge of Him, makes me free;

And with travailing resolve and prevailing chatter,

I call on Him, whose help really matters:

Matters of the heart which unveil all possessions,

Things true to my thoughts, and hearts confession;

Things held onto for so very long,

Now discovered, simply do not belong;

I saw in His kindness, all that I thought,

That Christ in all things already wrought;

Everything important or not, It's true,

What was done already, makes everything new:

I accept His will and desire over me,

To establish His working, what Himself does decree;

So I'll not argue what's resolved from Eternity lasting,

Not at all You see, for it's life everlasting.

So now I stand with renewed resolve,

In a new relationship to evolve;

A new and fresh breath, a blasting;

Set to discover the great life, a new tasking:

A covenant of timeless relationship,

measured in truth, strengthened in fellowship;

An abounding grace of beauty renewed,
With him no limits, Free... never subdued:

Who could believe that in time advancing,
It was nothing less than joyful romancing;
But in this fellowship, with Him contrasting,
Is peace and joy and love everlasting?

A MARRIAGE SONG

I heard in my spirit a resonant sound,

Melodies and combinations, A love song, newly found;

Two hearts beating with a fresh new tune,

Hurry next pressions and tailing lyrics loom:

A song of fragrant harmonies expressed,

By lives joined as one in sovereignty blessed;

Full with rhythmic inflection, Vast intonation,

A life of greater overture, interludes and orchestrations:

Many continuous works, And Esther and her king,

Flowered and sanded with hazelnut in Spring;

The scepter of romance, A continual concert,

Much resolved with intimate detail, A special dessert;

With sugared delight, sounds Especially vocal,

Voiced composition by poems in choral;

Harmonies, toned accord,
Qualities of singing, percussions and chords:

Like instruments playing, interludes of life, song,
A theater of musicians and chorus belongs;
Two lives in paraquet., staged as one,
Arranged together from time begun;

How will they fare and what do they sing,
Only fullness and no inhibitions to bring;
Coming together orchestrations to complete,
Undeniable, wonders, together forever replete.:

Musical instruments with concerto's of sounds,
Expediently lifted, numerically bound;
Abounding together in every voiced wail;
With glorious accompaniment of musical detail;

It's a song of marriage, and a song of two,

Becoming one and creating the new;

Statements of melodious and glamorous refrain,

That only life itself can ever explain.

FOUNDATIONS

What is this we see in the start of things?
How does it command the service it brings?
Even in the evolving of nations,
Nothing is truer than what's in the foundation;

It's the basis for what can exist,
No notion for differences and irrevocable Twists;
But holds its ground and settles down there,
To stabilize and hold true with resilient flair;

How is it enamored with the things it can do,
That is, Be the basis for everything true;
Would you think it's such a lowly place, without honor?
When the truth is, it's specially garnered;

The support for every purpose under the sun,
The strength of every building when it's begun;

The power to hold fast and to keep its Function,
in scriptural terms, it has holy unction;

Isn't it the base upon which things stand?
The provision for future maintenance given in hand;
Funds that grant the perpetual support.,
A foundation garment, endowments of cosmetic import;

Yes, it is the basis upon which everything stands,
Whether things in this country or in other lands;
Concepts, and ideas, inventions and the like,
To have no true foundation is surely to slight;

So then in every context we can see the need,
To embrace the foundation that makes things to be;
According to that which is built there on,
Able to endure and continue on;

Without fear of failure You see, or even stress of worry,

Because solid is the rock, that establishes the story;

To the end it will endure, to the end it will last,

Because with true foundation it holds fast.

_____

_____

_____

_____

_____

_____

_____

_____

_____

SACRIFICES

So often it's misunderstood or unrecognized,

The state of things that appear having been disguised;

The acts or the offerings of something to another,

A gift of homage paid, given in faith and no bother;

Are they always seen in the terms easily understood come? Are they accounted in the cost, For the common good;

What is the extremity of the money given or the time spent? The sacrifices made with judicious intent:

To avail our hearts to something and make it known,

To gain understanding in the things not shown;

Or to experience some measure of Wisdom's depth,

Or a light hearted song, a canzonet?

What can be the extent of that which is given?

How is it measured and by what is it driven?

Is it received with vagary or as a solemn work?

Where responsibility lies and duties not shirked?

It's not a capricious mind that we lend,

Or foolishness of heart and will that We tend;

But desires sincere and truly of value and worth,

Ordered an intent and made calmly as it comes forth;

Before feature of time in all its values.,

Yet, at times it seems to be very true;

For of him with whom we have to do, his image and his face;

We need his mercy and His abiding grace:

For the life of me, It seemed so hard,

But to wait before Him will show our reward;

I know it well in many a venue,

That what we give up in sacrifice, brings us through;

Not because we have bought our way out,

but because that he alone is what the sacrifice is about;
His will formed in you. And his will formed in me,
That's the only way we'll ever be free:

So stand the test and keep the faith,
Endure the trial, and watch his grace;
For the sufficient for the days ahead,
He will keep his word and do all that, he said;

As for me and for all of you,
Sacrifices for him is the least we can do;
The inquiries of heart that we can make,
Will leave our enemies trembling and cause them to quake;

Our sacrifices made is only a small part,
For what we desire of him, is really smart;
We give up that we value and all that we claim;
That we may possess Him and His righteous name.

WISDOM

Spirit Truth says; wisdom is justified of all Her children,
In the courses of life, we find many conditions then;
Each day the demand for greater understanding,
A prelude to circumstances, and needs commanding:

But what of this way of to do and to have,
Can it always account for the here and the now;
here and now, What do you mean?
That experience of faith to which we cling;

It is the expression of virtue made clear,
when the power of understanding brings us near;
we can savor the depths of wisdoms power, end game, victories
and blessings when others cowards;

For the fear of not knowing what they should do,
Leaves them broken, no hope, without clue;
Yeah, For all those who fail to embrace Her you see,
They are driven with Life's fullness of uncertainty;

The win against all conditions, The victory crown,
While their enemies sneer and fall to the ground;
Broken and completely in dismay,
They have no ready virtue that is able to sway;

So how do we get such an awesome grace?
How do we achieve this wonderful place?
To what or to whom do we assign such a task?
Where do we go, and whom shall we ask?

For such. A. A strengthened. Powerful plea,
Make us know wisdom with all its decrees;
Will it sustain us and will it last?

Only when we know him, Who all creation hast;

You see, it's not some mythical quality that we seek,
nor is it a place or time whereof we speak;
It is a person that we come to know,
whose breath on us as a great wind blows;

It is the greatness of him which we long for,
The strength and character of the sovereign Lord;
I know that in him we will find the key,
Ask, and it shall be given is his command You see;

And how shall we receive such an auspicious gift?
When we. To hear my hearts do lift;
with ready acceptance of the things he says,
and the obedience to carry out what before us, He lays;

So can we now say that the greater praise,
Is when to hear my R will we raise;

And trusting him that he knows the way,

He gives us grace to face the day;

Having this clarity and knowledge of Him

That what he gives us. Is his wisdom.

WISDOM AND AUTHORITY

When looking into liberties, perfect law,
Searching the wisdom, exposing the flaws;
What is determined where is its authority.
Or is authority itself the real liberty?

Looking again to see. It's pointing,
Its limits removed, the precious anointing;
Connected in place to break the yoke,
With grace and power., Unlimited strokes;

So how do they come together, How do they connect?
What's their pleasure? What can we expect?
The power of authority and the anointing;
How do they fit together? In pursuit, Unrelenting?

When authority is set in its special place,
it brings all things ordered and face to face;

Anointing comes and gives its blessing too,

Setting new limits and establishing the true;

Authority speaks, you see, words of direction,

Anointing brings us its fervent protection;

Strongholds removed in darkness, destroyed,

Together as one, in Loves power employed;

Authority established in revelations song,

Whose truths uncovers every certain wrong;

To the vengeance of anointings magnificent power,

The gentle sweetness of a perfect Flower;

Tending upon horizons beauty,

Lifting up anointing, settling with acuity;

Keenness of insights, direct and sharp,

Played as melodies up on the harp;A sound of wondrous and glorious praise,

As they come together with new levels to raise;

Experiencing such wonder and dramatic impact,
New consciousness raised and fellowship intact;

And finally then, when all is done,
As a new liberty is established and more victories won;
The authority rises with. Anointing, perceived,
And anointing settles within His depths received;

To bring the full of everything desired,
a quality of agreement in the new passions, tried;
A journey of relationship and expectations be done,
With wholeness and completeness becoming one:

_____
_____
_____
_____
_____
_____
_____

WHAT'S NEXT?

Considering everything that's been said and done,

The works of the day and the new life begun;

Or is it new?, or the continuation of the same?

With further expressions of impassioned flame;

A fire of new dimensions of Restorative Grace,

settling in to establish a different place;

For when the journey began it was unassured,

That we could walk in the same place without being lured;
Authority established.

Into a new dynamic of faith and commitment.,

A president called to. Greater involvements;

Places of virtue and love, set free,

to express itself in you and me;

Yes, you and me in a maze of hope and relief,

To seek to the end the spirits crease;

The one that leads to the expected end,

where we were meant to be pronounced and then;

Completely unveiled with the hope of His glory,

Because it was already spoken in the end of the story;

And what was said from the beginning must surely be,

This is what we desire; In this we are free:

So, Speaking of his will in the proper context,

Allows us to see what we can expect next;

That the spirit of him will do as it will,

To take us through and over each hill;

Into the valleys and out again,

As a guide and instructor, a blessed friend;

We will not agonize over the way that we go,

Because with certainty, the mystery is known by the one who knows.

We are not confused in this. We've seen,

It's been very clear and made us to dream;

of all its possibilities and endless limits,

So to the journey given we will commit;

Can anything be too hard for God?

Who brought us to the time of this sod?

Too hard for him who all life gives,

And chooses now for us to live;

We live in this life as well as the next,

and this is everything that we have come to expect;

So joyfully we trod and stay the course,

proceeding in him without remorse;

Without sullenness but sober and true,

Who we serve with him with whom we have to do;

knowing for certain that we are highly blessed,

And can endure in the process, even in what is next:

IN THE MIDNIGHT HOUR

I shudder to think of what goes On,

In the hour of darkness, from midnight to dawn;

The time when things hit and come forth,

Actions of those who seek darkness' reward;

Times of evil when hearts do seek,

To find their way into the desires that reek;

Of lust and sin a treasured cove,

Lusciousness and revelries A demented trove;

Sprites that operate to sustain their pleasure, Detestable workings and vehement measure;

What can destroy such demonstrative matters?

Breaking of yokes and strongholds with rigorous splatter;

None but the righteous working in love with faith,

Can destroy the workings of evils wrath;

Prayer made and praise is given,

By those who worship with their spirit driven;

To produce the light in works made clear,

as they seek for truth in obedience, dear;

Given to standards of truth and love,

Being wise as serpents, yet harmless as doves;

Who is the one who can establish the cause,

war without distraction and take no pause?

You are one if you accept the call,

I the other, we refuse to fall;

Victims to the night in aberrant sleaze,

But faithful. And true together we please;

in prayerful virtue and aggressive works,

we minister together as Kingdom clerks;

Assign to be Marshalls of truth,

Working in course are Destiny's tribute;
In acts of authority and power you see,
even in the midnight hour, holding degree;

Degrees of integrity and honor, for sure,
Under all circumstances at stabilizing core;
Whether in the daytime or in the night,
Staying focused and diligent to fight;

Knowing that in no uncertain terms,
we've come to carry out the assigned, the affirmed;
By the Spirit of God we carry the mantle,
And do all that's well, no part to dangle:

But faithful and true, do give proper expression,
To the hours we serve, an excellent confession;
So who can know what else to do?
Truth is, it's our choice and all up to me and you.

HEARTBEATS

Trump, Thump, thump; The pounding melodies Expressive sound,

Stirrings and churnings with intimacy found;

Lie the flow of waters. Thundering falls,

Energized by Gravity's pool and Hurricane Squalls;

Heartbeats together in a flow, oneness;

Caressing each other with rhythmic fondness,

Measured in sensations of rhythmic tents,

A rhyme explicit in poetic license;

Beatings, Stirrings, intimation without fear,

Explosive with emotions, expectant, and clear;

The dryness of voice and waterless pate,

As to the intended purposes of Glorious fate;

gradual building of racing hearts,

Burning together, blending as one; while losing no part;

Crystalline color, then abounding true,

Uncompromised, answering each call; Heartbeats, renewed:

What of this bond, What of its Glue?

How do they mesh and what's their clue?

That they have what it takes,

One together, no whim nor flakes Can they be approved in the place they give seat?

True to their destiny as one heartbeat;

I know, so in the heart of me,

as I wonder awed, with the intensity;

The thoughts that lie within my spirit,

Sensitive to their very need, I hear it;

No longer left with doubts that roar,

Or words that dangle on a distant shore;

but simply this knowledge of that which? Is to come,

As we travel together having already won;

Because the heart of me that beats in you,
beats to the reason of all that's true;
For the measure of the sound is not my own,
But the sound of him expressed and known;

This heart also beats in the depths of you,
It confirms his presence and workings too;
So how do we fail when we can hear his heart?
He's the sum total of every?

That has to do with us you see,
Two hearts in one, and his makes three;
This is the wisdom of the One Who Knows,
hearts beating together and their glory shows;

That what has been given is still replete,
With His expression as one heartbeat.

THE CHAMBER

Quickly engulfed through the night. Sweet caress,

Wanton with experience, Impassioned and dressed;

With the linen of righteousness they waited their time,

And found the pleasure of intimacy, specially primed:

Ohh, flow of water that visibly stands,

They know in their actions, what they can command;

How can they know what they will do,

When they are called in trial? A test to construe;

The purpose for which our Christ gained the bride,

and set in place is glorious stride;

The colors of joy and the prisms of light,

Which Compel hearts to enter the fight;

The Fight of faith and the Enduring of tests,

which prove with confidence. We are his best;

That can honor and adore in a radiant peace,

Show forth his greatness with actions Which speak;

Toiling victor vigorously, and the static with desire,

Impassioned and genuine with Holy Fire;

Basking in sunlight and the starlights glow,

With the morning dew and springs that flow:

To fulfill the call and the relative experience,

that grants to us life's wondrous radiance;

The travails of struggle that reveal the war,

Against the righteous And what's in store;

We who love to show our worth,

In the inner places of virtues, warmth;

The chambers of intimacy, open and free,

Against the righteous, And what's in store;

We who live to show our worth,

in the inner places of virtues, warmth;
The Chamber of intimacy, open and free,
producing the joy of union; Life's jubilee:
No longer captive to the thoughts of the mind,
but fully released into a transforming kind:

Of oneness and aspiring through mutual benefit,
Steaming in the soothing piece of No limits;
compelled by the certainty of truth released,
my words confessed, then singleness deceased:

So see the tangible and transforming,
Work of relationship and the spirit performing;
His desire and works attesting,
Because the chamber is open and it's flavor professing;

The fragrance of the flower Candled.,
Supports the ambient sensations that can't be handled;
By the mere wisdoms of natural thought,

For the expense of the chamber and what is bought;

knowing this, that the things produced,
are greater measure than what's reduced;
So setting the heart to know the call,
Is chambered in layers and revealed in all;

Those who desire and know and will not chide,
but stay steadfast in their will to abide;
expressing the merit of jubilant revelations,
with total resolve to have chambers manifestation;

So what is chamber? A Crucible of sorts;
A place of Release, Stability, and Heavenly courts;
A new found expression of passions revealed,
as an orange in sections and freshly peeled;

It is the place of mystery made open to their hearts,
and brought into focus through the sum of the parts;

Only the man and the woman can know,

That the chamber opens and gives the full show:

So do not doubt its worth and cost,

Because the chamber is established, so none is lost.

MORE THAN JUST WORDS

It appears to me that much in life can be estranged,

Persuade us against the willing change,

the place of peace we can enjoy,

But loses its zeal in distant ploys;

Of obvious exposures to words of mistrust,

And Quicken in us disturbing disgust;

The things we see but don't respect,

And how they measure to standards we protect;

So what do we do to compensate,

when desire is lost to participate?;

With those whose words seem never true,

and the lies they tell and misconstrue;

The purposes and the intent for all things right,

but failed to stand and overcome each plight;

Can such an one ever be trusted?

When there have been workings that left you busted:

I think it difficult at best,

to recognize the obvious test.;

That life is fleeting and time is short,

\That it must not be considered. Has only sport;

But all that is given for destiny's peace,

And established in timing to bring release;

To order its steps and set its pace,

That we observe and face to face;

So nothing that others can do or say,

can determine your words and how you sway;

But you alone, to what Is right, be true,

And it's the only thing that you can do;

Go allows you to stand in life's glory,

Experiencing its joy in a brand new story;

Who can tell its wondrous charms?
It's energies released and availing alarms:

Too things new that continually refreshes,
To walk out in vigorous and revealing threshes;
Of mystery and exciting Intrigues,
Left exhausted, at times, even emotionally fatigued.

Yet new on the Morrow, and we confess the truth,
We speak. It starts and carries through;
We command the words that declare its good,
It leaves us encouraged, and, well, it should:

For the words we speak, Minister Life,
they lessen the futility of distressing strife;
The words give life by what we communicate,
Go to anticipates our destiny as we participate:

We are what we say when we speak from the heart,

Often it's difficult or course to chart;

Yes, our words give a clue to who we are,

And magnifies where we come to and just how far:

So when the Lies. Are told they give insight,

To the places we live in and just how Trite;

Within declare the need to speak,

And to say our peace or so we leak:

Through the expressions of what lies innermost,

And the course we tread That borders are coasts;

So we see clearly what? Our borders,

and the words give us the limits and marching orders:

So guard your words and what you say,

They give the full intent of each day;

Keep what you speak and command your peace,

With the words of life express your belief.

HIM

I Fail at times to understand,

The full intent of the Masters plan;

A plan so complete and vast to me,

But fully known to him, you see;

A plan established from the end,

And set in place to accomplish and then;

Settled deep in the heart of Him,

Each part revealed, its purpose with vin;

The vigor and zeal is to make sure it may,

You as well and not for free;

You and I can serve without charge,

As circumstances evolve and upon us barge;

Into all affairs as hungry intrusions,

Eating our fabric and causing confusions;

But arrested by trust for His words and regard,
Like bits and pieces of broken shards;

Yet, Christ with us, whose glory unfolds;
Making known for certain, His sure cause,
With no notions of taking a pause;

His will goes on in every way,
And we search for it our price to pay;
The expense of walking in all alignment,
Often though confounded, and without understanding.
Seeking to find a permanent landing.

A place familiar to us and yet,
His ways are beyond ours and so we fret;
At times while expecting handsome rewards,
But is it anything we can afford?

The only hope I can believe,

Is that in all I will, He can retrieve;

The sum of all that was prepared before,

Confident that He can handle each chore;

For all that is done will yet be His,

And from our task He will not fiz

But true to His word I am assured,

That nothing less can He afford;

W know this truth and with me understand,

He cannot fail in His master plan;

Take comfort with me in all of this,

That the all wise God who cannot lie, cannot miss.

_____
_____
_____
_____
_____

I SEE THE TIME

I see the move of time on lives,
Living in breaches of 9 to 5;
Limited in the total plan,
Where men are called to full intent, to stand;

Compelled to works that cannot do,
What is necessary and what is true;
That is to say that there is a place,
Where the need is greater but still we waste;

Our efforts and all our energy,
On things that steal time and won't set free;
Our hearts and minds from useless dribbles,
Of futility made known and times that cripple;

How do we see the time we have?
As mice in a lab or meat on the butcher's slab;

In the context of all that is of no use,

We become as dung in the dumps of refuse;

How do we see time as the endless commodity?

With no understanding of it's mystery,

That there are days and months and years;

And what we lose in wasted effort brings sullen tears:

Can we again what we have lost?;

Minutes and seconds of time that cost,

Us precious chronos and how we fail,

Because we do not have and thus we wail;

With tears of hurt and extravagant loss,

Enshrouded with the cocoon of life's albatross;

Which flies in the sky and stills not our fear,

Because we call it a curse of visions lost and dear;

Forsaken times of hope and peace,

For we see no end and sweet release;

The times of destiny fulfilled and grand,
The courageous alignments of success we plan;
It's evidence seen the place we stand,
Giving us satisfaction of the highest brand;

Yet we see that there is a place of grace,
Which restores our hope and keeps the pace;
With what we have been called to do in this time,
And will not lose and is made divine;

For we keep not the path in vain you see,
That expresses the call for you and me;
The assertion of a greater will,
That places all things in order still;

Against all works of flesh and sensitivity,
To the will of men who seek their destiny;
A desire to do inspite of what erupts,

And under no circumstances will they give up;

So look and see what time affords,
Submit your will, become one accord;
With the strength of truth that itself avails,
Wisdoms understanding and what it's; hail?

Open and daunting in full commitment,
It brings the completing of all investment;
Rewards of fervor and passion of living,
All revealed in time with mutual giving;

Then look and see what time does offer,
And fill your trove and line your coffers;
It's the blessing of knowing all that time bring,
And to it all let your soul then cling;

Not to stuff but to purpose in you,
And time will abide and not misconstrue;

But give to you your appointed share,

With the guarantee to all that it will not spare;

But release in you the measure of itself,

And raise your standard to the highest shelf;

To bring it all to fruitful ends,

And then another time to start again.

INTIMATELY

Strange the word that approaches me,

My heart compelled to look and see;

What is produced when time is spent,

And how it operates and what is meant;

When we speak of it's desire and passions renewed,

How it is established and how it is viewed,

In the heart of those who seek it's charms

Coming away spent in wonderous alarms;

With purposed torrents of love's display,

Stirred in full confidence that it has it's way;

Of involving in us every part,

Without divulging it's bitter sweet tarts;

For you can not taste of intimacy,

And everything that it will plea;

And not be involved with all it's sensitivities,

With inflections and it's proclivities;

So we seek then to taste the depth of her,

Every crease and every curr;

For the sum of it is based in all,

The hidden, the seen, the great and the small;

So would you look only to that which pleases?

Would you believe that only certain areas have increases,

The depth and the quality of the intimate detail,

Or the rapid symmetry's of the whole of it's spells?

Can it be that you must touch it all?

That you must answer the question and it's calls,

For in openness of spirit and with earnest plea,

That it may avail itself so that you can see;

That what it possesses is not for all eyes,

But for the ones who honestly tries;

To know what is under the surface and so much more,

And are resolute to pursue till they settle the score;

That is to say that to know the history,

It's treasured and benefits, it's constant mystery;

And what will it show and how much can it free,

To the heart of the one who seeks intimately.

_____
_____
_____
_____
_____
_____
_____
_____
_____
_____

I TRIED TO KNOW

I wanted to understand the mystery that loomed,
The sudden loss of vision in the blossom bloomed;
Or was it just a consequence of the unknown,
That kept the rose from being fully blown;

Into the full of the call, the place of destiny,
That releases one to be everything they could be;
The measured and constrained of life subtlety's
With definitions set for the total history;

Yet to be made manifest in quickened pace.
A hastening to perform in the assigned space;
Uninhibited by the mind of men and given liberty,
To express the purposes of all, that this flower is intended to be;

It has in it the beauty and yet the thorn,
The character of the seed explained and born;

To carry the traits of it's witness with complete confidence,
But in the whole of itself, it is still condensed;

Not because of any limits that one can see,
But because it's needed the pollinations of the bee;
To transfer the grains that inseminate,
And bring to life and to impregnate;

What of the process that is given to all,
I tried to see what could cause such a fall;
The struggles which beset the heart,
That take their toll's in life and leave their mark:

What is their insistence and how they are comprised,
The completeness of their intent in desires derived;
Hunger to serve itself and not the common good,
For what it was intimated and what it should;

How does it come to this?

What makes the flower it's mark to miss?

Was it the heat of the Sun?

Burning away the root in the process begun:

Or the lack of the intimate water,

Which gives it life and nurtures without bother;

As that not intending to steal and take,

Recognizing everything within that's at stake:

But pushes to release the full potential,

Making everything else seem consequential;

And each thought of it misunderstood,

As breaches of the will assert their own good:

Whose fault and what's to blame?

Can only be revealed in the heart's own shame;

At knowing that it did not grow or receive the report,

That gave it's quality and to the mark came short;

Still, there is a hope that in the midst of it all.

What did not stand will hear again it's call;

That it will respond to the voice of destiny's sound,

And will live again and in true purpose; abound.

_____
_____
_____
_____
_____
_____
_____
_____
_____
_____
        _____

CONSUMMATION

So I saw the need to speak to her,

An urgency in my spirit, my will concurred;

Tell Her what you know is true today,

I felt pressed to give Her what I had to say;

It was a great And personal lingering,

And staying focused In the subject and triggering;

Passions and desires in the depth of my soul,

And only the truth made known could make me whole;

So I said to Her what I should in all my expressions,

Believing that there could be no depression;

As I made known the secrets of my will,

And I trusted Her that she would understand and still;

Would believe that it was a placer she could trust,

It would not damage Her nor Her heart would bust;

As she came to this place of the knowledge of me,
And allowed Herself to gain such distinct intimacy;

A place that she had secured with no intent that was Her own,
yet, come to possess and had not till then known;
How had this happened and what will be it's end?
Time will show and days will tell what is to come and then;

Give it's evidence explicit and in totality,
Leaving us in possession of loves' stability;
Granting the joy of reverent summation,
When we come together in holy consummation;

Consummation of the union that pleases,
It's very impressions of gratuitous releases;
Bringing the fullness of benefit and glorious completions,
Dispelling all myths of the relationships untimely deletion:
For it is not what others said or others think,
This is the cup of blessing we're given to drink;

A tasteful delight of unfailing blessing,
And love's own will, it's delight expressing:

So we take the time to walk out the true,
And watch for the loss of the old and giving of the new;
Undisturbed and other's portent,
But faithful to that, which is the original intent:

So come to me my love and trust my will,
That the grace is given and time will seal;
Our expectation for all in culmination,
As we enter together into our consummation.

_____
_____
_____
_____
_____
_____
_____

OUR WEDDING NIGHT

At midnight she is gathered by her beloved,

With mission and purpose; a spirit dove;

He comes as one obsessed,

For His betrothed, a full desire to bless;

She steals away with Him, with Her dove eyes,

She is confident that in truth he tells no lies;

Her heart is beating fierce and strong,

And to Him alone she now belongs;

She is drunken with love's wine and pow poured out in Her desire,

How and when did He kindle such fire;

It was when He laid His thoughts in the breasts of Her,

He speaks Her name; she drips with the oil of myrrh;

So His fruit is pleasant and sweet to taste,

Her heart pounds fierce with expectant haste;

She thinks of Him a tree of apple tucked in her backwoods,

And She knows that she's sustained with His gentle good;

So He plans His way in loving desire,

To warm Himself in her intimate fires;

That in the night course you see,

To minister pleasant life to Her; to unveil Her mysteries;

She is ravaged then with His love,

He caresses Her gently as the fairest dove;

Now when the joy of that night comes to dawn,

Her garments scented as the smells, O' Cedars of Lebanon;

And gathered now has been the tokens,

Which tell of night sounds and glories unspoken;

She will be still with the presence of wonders light,

As she hears of new things and lives that shine bright;

Where two have become one,

In a journey now newly begun.

OUR WEDDING RING

Small the band with metals, Precious and spent,

Gold or silver, our wedding ring;

Having jewels of glorious intent,

A sound, a tone that sings;

Curious that sound, A circular movement,

A Symphony of orchestration and dance;

Two hearts united to give forth a clear sound….oneness,

Their will and spirits lanced;

A set together, one operation,

A man, a woman, addition or multiplication?

The character: quality? Especially whose perceptions ring true,

A bell, a chime with moments ringing;

Each one God breathed and new,

The ring which leads in course…a circle;

The unctions gentle and sweet,

A holy union before God and man;

A wonderous journey to complete

So with all desire and holy vision;

With grateful heart for new days ahead,

While breaking the Hymen and circumcision;

With this ring I thee wed!

SPECIAL

How can I say what is happening to my heart?

What words are there that can tell,

I try to speak and to say my part,

And in reserve, I try not to yell;

And what shall I speak that expresses my thought?

The intimate of me, to you,

The desires I have and how I've fought,

How can I prove that they are true?

I care so deeply for the one I see,

With life's eyes wide open and clear;

And the churning of my spirit and words that flee,

And how I'm longing to have you near;

I guess that somehow I must find a way,

And do it with the sum of me;

Speak to you each and every day,
How your care and friendship, makes me free!!

Made in the USA
Columbia, SC
04 December 2024